DENVER BRONCOS

BRENDAN FLYNN

WWW.APEXEDITIONS.COM

Copyright © 2025 by Apex Editions, Mendota Heights, MN 55120. All rights reserved. No part of this book may be reproduced or utilized in any form or by any means without written permission from the publisher.

Apex is distributed by North Star Editions:
sales@northstareditions.com | 888-417-0195

Produced for Apex by Red Line Editorial.

Photographs ©: Ryan Kang/AP Images, cover, 1; Justin Edmonds/Getty Images Sport/Getty Images, 4–5, 46–47; Justin Tafoya/Getty Images Sport/Getty Images, 6–7; Bettmann/Getty Images, 8–9; Jerry Mosey/AP Images, 10–11; Focus On Sport/Getty Images Sport/Getty Images, 12–13, 22–23; George Gojkovich/Getty Images Sport/Getty Images, 14–15; Allen Kee/Getty Images Sport/Getty Images, 16–17; David Durochik/AP Images, 19, 57; Clifton Boutelle/Getty Images Sport/Getty Images, 20–21; Al Bello/Allsport/Getty Images Sport/Getty Images, 24–25; William R. Sallaz/Getty Images Sport/Getty Images, 26–27; Brian Bahr/Allsport/Getty Images Sport/Getty Images, 29; Paul Spinelli/AP Images, 30–31, 58–59; Doug Pensinger/Getty Images Sport/Getty Images, 32–33, 42–43; Greg Trott/AP Images, 34–35; Michael Owens/Getty Images Sport/Getty Images, 36–37; Don Juan Moore/Getty Images Sport/Getty Images, 39; Thearon W. Henderson/Getty Images Sport/Getty Images, 40–41; Dilip Vishwanat/Getty Images Sport/Getty Images, 44–45; Brian Bahr/Getty Images Sport/Getty Images, 48–49; Dustin Bradford/Icon Sportswire, 50–51; Dustin Bradford/Getty Images Sport/Getty Images, 52–53; Kevin Reece/Getty Images Sport/Getty Images, 54–55

Library of Congress Control Number: 2023922214

ISBN
979-8-89250-151-4 (hardcover)
979-8-89250-168-2 (paperback)
979-8-89250-292-4 (ebook pdf)
979-8-89250-185-9 (hosted ebook)

Printed in the United States of America
Mankato, MN
012025

NOTE TO PARENTS AND EDUCATORS

Apex books are designed to build literacy skills in striving readers. Exciting, high-interest content attracts and holds readers' attention. The text is carefully leveled to allow students to achieve success quickly.

TABLE OF CONTENTS

CHAPTER 1
MILE HIGH 4

CHAPTER 2
EARLY HISTORY 8

PLAYER SPOTLIGHT
JOHN ELWAY 18

CHAPTER 3
LEGENDS 20

PLAYER SPOTLIGHT
TERRELL DAVIS 28

CHAPTER 4
RECENT HISTORY 30

PLAYER SPOTLIGHT
VON MILLER 38

CHAPTER 5
MODERN STARS 40

CHAPTER 6
TEAM TRIVIA 48

TEAM RECORDS • 56
TIMELINE • 58
COMPREHENSION QUESTIONS • 60
GLOSSARY • 62
TO LEARN MORE • 63
ABOUT THE AUTHOR • 63
INDEX • 64

CHAPTER 1
MILE HIGH

It's a crisp fall afternoon. Denver Broncos fans fill the stadium. Suddenly, a white horse races onto the field. The team's players follow closely behind. The crowd goes wild. It's time for football!

The Broncos have sold out every home game since 1970.

The horse's name is Thunder. He is the Broncos' mascot. And his day is just getting started. Soon, Denver scores. Thunder runs from one end zone to the other. He does that for every Broncos touchdown.

FAMOUS STADIUM

Denver is known as the Mile High City. That's because the city is one mile above sea level. The Broncos' first stadium was called Mile High Stadium. The team moved into a new stadium in 2001. Many fans call it New Mile High.

Broncos players celebrate a touchdown during a 2023 game against the Kansas City Chiefs.

CHAPTER 2

EARLY HISTORY

The Denver Broncos began playing in 1960. They were part of the AFL. This league was separate from the NFL. The Broncos struggled at first. In 1960, they had the worst record in the AFL.

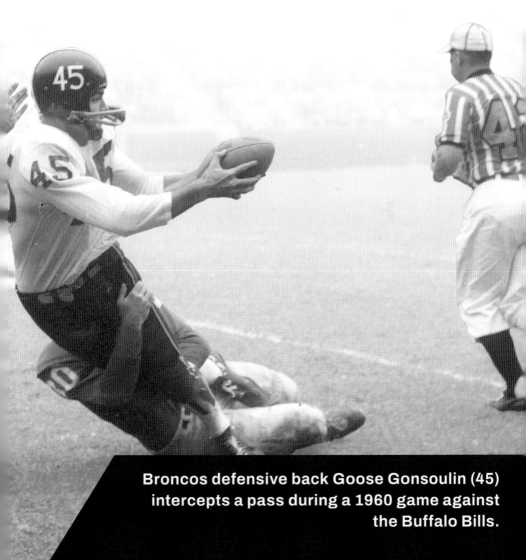

Broncos defensive back Goose Gonsoulin (45) intercepts a pass during a 1960 game against the Buffalo Bills.

Denver quarterback Frank Tripucka runs for a touchdown against the New York Titans in 1962.

Things didn't improve much over the next few seasons. The Broncos won just two games in 1963. They matched that record the next year. In 1970, the AFL and NFL joined together. But Denver's struggles continued.

STRANGE UNIFORMS

The Broncos had some strange uniforms in their early years. The team's colors were brown and yellow. And the socks had vertical stripes. In 1962, Denver changed its colors to orange and blue. The team burned the old uniforms.

In 1977, the Broncos reached the playoffs for the first time. And they didn't stop there. In the first round, they beat the Pittsburgh Steelers. Next, they beat the Oakland Raiders. That sent the Broncos to the Super Bowl. In the big game, Denver fell to the Dallas Cowboys. Even so, it was a great season.

ORANGE CRUSH

In 1977, Denver's defense was known for crushing its opponents. And the team's jerseys were bright orange. So, fans started calling the Broncos' defenders the "Orange Crush." The name came from a soda that was popular at the time.

Rob Lytle (41) scored Denver's only touchdown in the Super Bowl against the Cowboys.

In 1983, Denver traded for rookie quarterback John Elway. He quickly became the greatest player in team history. Elway led the Broncos to three Super Bowls in the 1980s. However, Denver lost all three.

THE DRIVE

In the 1986 season, Denver reached the conference championship game. The Cleveland Browns led 20–13. Less than six minutes remained. Denver got the ball at its own 2-yard line. Elway marched the offense 98 yards. With 31 seconds left, he threw a touchdown pass. Denver won the game in overtime.

John Elway (7) scans the field during a playoff game against the Cleveland Browns.

Terrell Davis (30) powers his way through Atlanta's defense during the Super Bowl.

In the 1997 season, Elway led his team back to the Super Bowl. This time, Denver came out on top. The Broncos shocked the Green Bay Packers. The next season, the Broncos won the Super Bowl again. They beat the Atlanta Falcons.

SHOCKING LOSS

In 1996, Denver had a 13–3 record. Many fans thought the team would finally win the Super Bowl. Instead, the Broncos suffered a tough loss in the playoffs. The Jacksonville Jaguars had been in the NFL for just two years. But they beat Denver 30–27.

PLAYER SPOTLIGHT

JOHN ELWAY

John Elway was a star quarterback at Stanford University. He was also a great baseball player. The Baltimore Colts selected Elway in the 1983 draft. But Elway didn't want to play for them. He said he would play pro baseball if the Colts didn't trade him.

Denver traded for the strong-armed rookie. It was the start of a 16-year career with the Broncos. Elway was the master of the late comeback. As long as he was in the game, the Broncos had hope. Elway led his team to 31 fourth-quarter comebacks.

JOHN ELWAY THREW 300 TOUCHDOWN PASSES IN HIS CAREER.

CHAPTER 3
LEGENDS

Wide receiver Lionel Taylor was Denver's first big star. He led the AFL in catches five times. Running back Floyd Little joined the team in 1967. Four seasons later, Little was the NFL's top rusher. Quarterback Craig Morton came to Denver in 1977. He took the Broncos to the Super Bowl that season.

Floyd Little (44) looks for extra yards during a 1972 game against the Cincinnati Bengals.

Lyle Alzado recorded 64.5 sacks during his eight years with the Broncos.

The Orange Crush defense carried the Broncos in the late 1970s. Lyle Alzado was one of its biggest stars. He was a fierce pass rusher. Linebacker Tom Jackson was a tackling machine. Later, linebacker Karl Mecklenburg took on a leadership role. He made the Pro Bowl six times during his 12-year career.

BREAKING BARRIERS

In the 1960s, Black players didn't get many chances to play quarterback. Marlin Briscoe helped change that. He started five games as a rookie in 1968. Briscoe was the first Black quarterback to start a game in the AFL or NFL.

Steve Atwater (27) returns an interception during a 1996 game.

Dennis Smith was the Broncos' top safety in the 1980s. He intercepted 30 passes in his career. In the 1990s, safety Steve Atwater led Denver's defense. He was one of the league's hardest hitters. Linebacker Bill Romanowski joined Denver in 1996. In his six seasons with the team, he recorded 433 tackles.

RETURN EXPERT

Punt returners don't always get much attention. But Rick Upchurch was a special case. In 1976, he returned four punts for touchdowns. That season, he led the NFL in punt return average. He led the league again in 1978 and 1982.

Shannon Sharpe caught 55 touchdown passes in his 12 seasons with Denver.

In the late 1990s, Denver had an amazing offense. Quarterback John Elway led the way. Tight end Shannon Sharpe was one of his favorite targets. Wide receiver Rod Smith also made lots of big plays. Running back Terrell Davis led the team's ground attack. Davis earned the Most Valuable Player (MVP) Award in 1998.

PLAYER SPOTLIGHT

TERRELL DAVIS

The Broncos drafted running back Terrell Davis in 1995. Few people expected much from him. He was a sixth-round pick. But Davis earned the starting job as a rookie. He ran for 1,117 yards that season.

Davis was just getting started. He improved his rushing totals in each of the next three seasons. In 1998, he ran for more than 2,000 yards. He was just the fourth player in NFL history to do that. A knee injury forced Davis to end his career early. But he still earned a spot in the Pro Football Hall of Fame.

TERRELL DAVIS LED THE NFL WITH 23 TOUCHDOWNS IN 1998.

CHAPTER 4

RECENT HISTORY

John Elway retired after winning his second Super Bowl. After that, the Broncos stumbled a bit. In 2005, Denver reached the conference title game. They fell to the Steelers. However, better times were ahead.

Running back Tatum Bell tries to break a tackle during the conference championship game of the 2005 season.

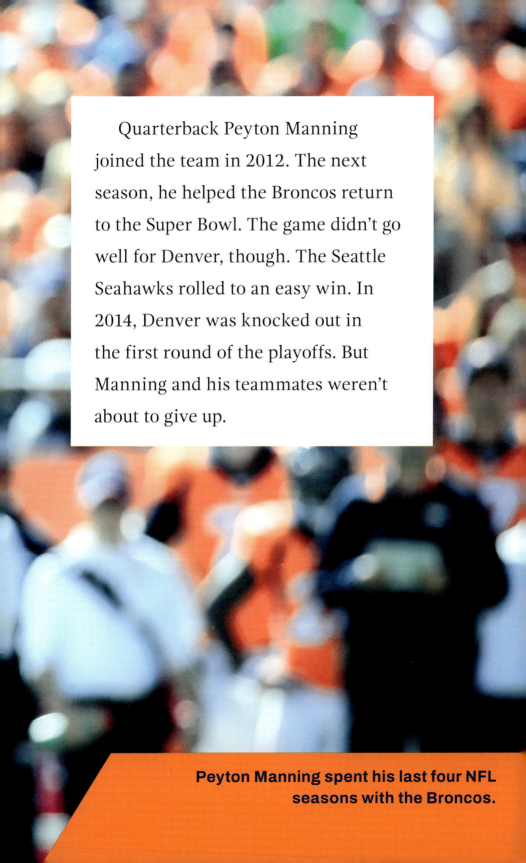

Quarterback Peyton Manning joined the team in 2012. The next season, he helped the Broncos return to the Super Bowl. The game didn't go well for Denver, though. The Seattle Seahawks rolled to an easy win. In 2014, Denver was knocked out in the first round of the playoffs. But Manning and his teammates weren't about to give up.

Peyton Manning spent his last four NFL seasons with the Broncos.

Von Miller (58) pursues Panthers quarterback Cam Newton during the Super Bowl.

In 2015, the Broncos won their division. Then they pulled out two close wins in the playoffs. Once again, Denver was in the Super Bowl. Manning and the Broncos beat the Carolina Panthers 24–10. It was Denver's third NFL title.

FROM BACKUP TO COACH

Gary Kubiak served as John Elway's backup for nine seasons. After he retired, he got into coaching. Kubiak spent many years as the Broncos' offensive coordinator. Then, in 2015, he took over as the team's head coach. In his first season, he led Denver to a Super Bowl win.

After Manning retired, the Broncos began a dry spell. The team went through lots of quarterbacks. But none of them had much success. Denver missed the playoffs several years in a row. In 2022, the team traded for quarterback Russell Wilson. But he was traded away after the 2023 season.

NEW COACH

Sean Payton spent many years coaching the New Orleans Saints. He helped them win a Super Bowl title in 2009. In 2023, Payton became Denver's new head coach. However, his first season was bumpy. The Broncos finished with a record of 8–9.

Russell Wilson threw for 6,594 yards in his two seasons with Denver.

PLAYER SPOTLIGHT

VON MILLER

The Broncos selected Von Miller in the 2011 draft. He quickly became one of the NFL's best pass rushers. Miller could dominate games. He racked up at least 10 sacks in seven of his first eight seasons.

Miller was at his best during important moments. In the 2015 conference title game, he came up big. He recorded 2.5 sacks and an interception. Two weeks later, Miller had another great game in the Super Bowl. Once again, he had 2.5 sacks. He also forced two fumbles. Miller was named the game's MVP.

VON MILLER'S 110.5 SACKS ARE THE MOST IN BRONCOS HISTORY.

CHAPTER 5
MODERN STARS

Peyton Manning had a great four-year run as Denver's quarterback. He set several NFL records during that time. In 2013, Manning threw 55 touchdown passes. That broke the old record of 50.

Peyton Manning (18) often changed plays at the line of scrimmage.

In the early 2010s, Demaryius Thomas caught 10 or more touchdown passes three years in a row.

Wide receiver Demaryius Thomas caught many of Manning's throws. Thomas hauled in 14 touchdown passes in 2013.

Courtland Sutton joined the Broncos in 2018. He became one of Denver's top receivers. In 2019, Sutton made his first Pro Bowl.

OMAHA!

Manning often lined up in the shotgun formation. When he wanted to change the play, he shouted "Omaha!" Manning said it so often that he became known for it. After Manning retired, he started a company. He called it Omaha Productions.

Elvis Dumervil (92) forced 16 fumbles in six seasons with Denver.

Elvis Dumervil had 63.5 sacks in six years with the Broncos. His best season came in 2009. He led the NFL with 17 sacks. Dumervil missed the next season due to injury. But when he returned, he teamed up with Von Miller. The pair was a nightmare for opposing teams.

GOING OUT ON TOP

Linebacker DeMarcus Ware spent most of his career with the Dallas Cowboys. During that time, he averaged 13 sacks per year. Ware joined the Broncos in 2014. And he was still a Pro Bowl defender. He also won his only Super Bowl ring with Denver.

Chris Harris (25) celebrates an interception during a 2017 game against the Dallas Cowboys.

Champ Bailey made plenty of big plays for the Broncos. In 2006, he led the NFL with 10 interceptions. After Bailey retired, Chris Harris became Denver's top cornerback. In his nine years with the team, he pulled down 20 interceptions. Cornerback Patrick Surtain II joined the Broncos in 2021. The next year, he made his first Pro Bowl.

FINISHING STRONG

Brian Dawkins was another Hall of Famer who spent the last years of his career in Denver. The longtime Philadelphia Eagles safety made the Pro Bowl twice as a Bronco. He averaged 78 tackles per season with the team.

CHAPTER 6
TEAM TRIVIA

In 1997, running back Terrell Davis started a new tradition. After his touchdowns, he began giving salutes. Sometimes he saluted his teammates. Other times, he saluted the fans. The celebration caught on quickly. It became known as the "Mile High Salute."

Terrell Davis (30) and Byron Chamberlain (86) give each other the Mile High Salute during a 1997 game.

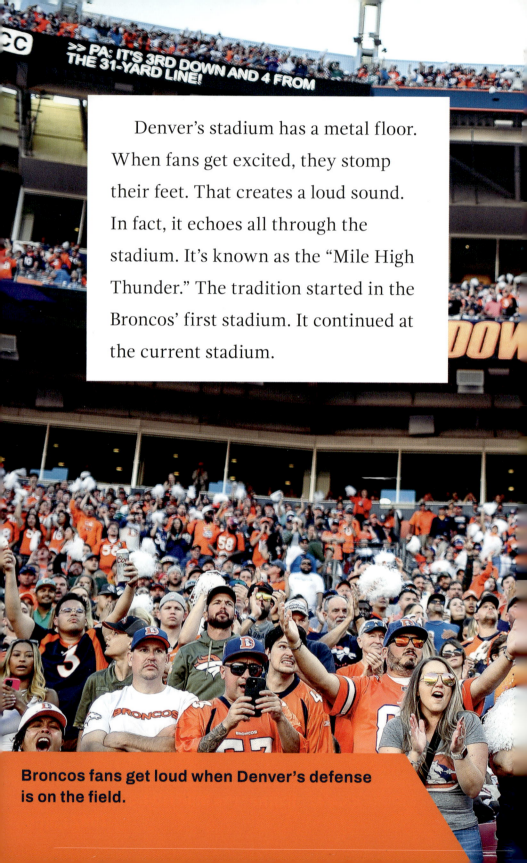

Denver's stadium has a metal floor. When fans get excited, they stomp their feet. That creates a loud sound. In fact, it echoes all through the stadium. It's known as the "Mile High Thunder." The tradition started in the Broncos' first stadium. It continued at the current stadium.

Broncos fans get loud when Denver's defense is on the field.

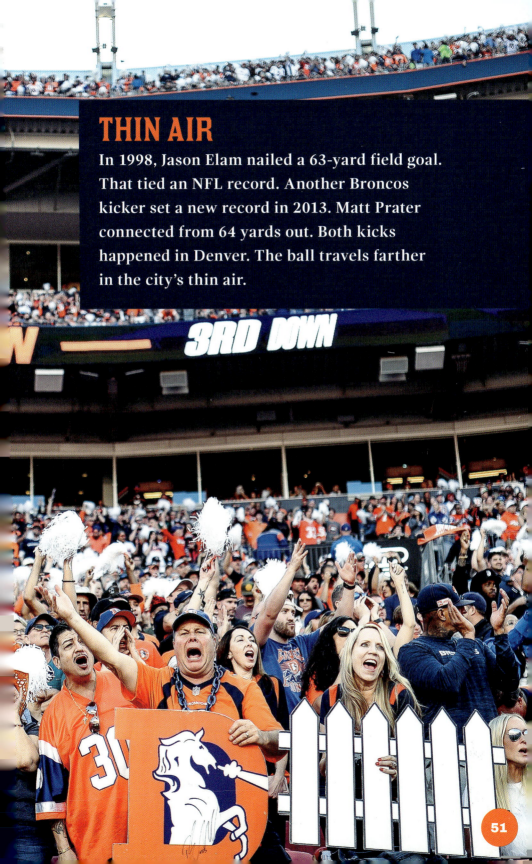

THIN AIR

In 1998, Jason Elam nailed a 63-yard field goal. That tied an NFL record. Another Broncos kicker set a new record in 2013. Matt Prater connected from 64 yards out. Both kicks happened in Denver. The ball travels farther in the city's thin air.

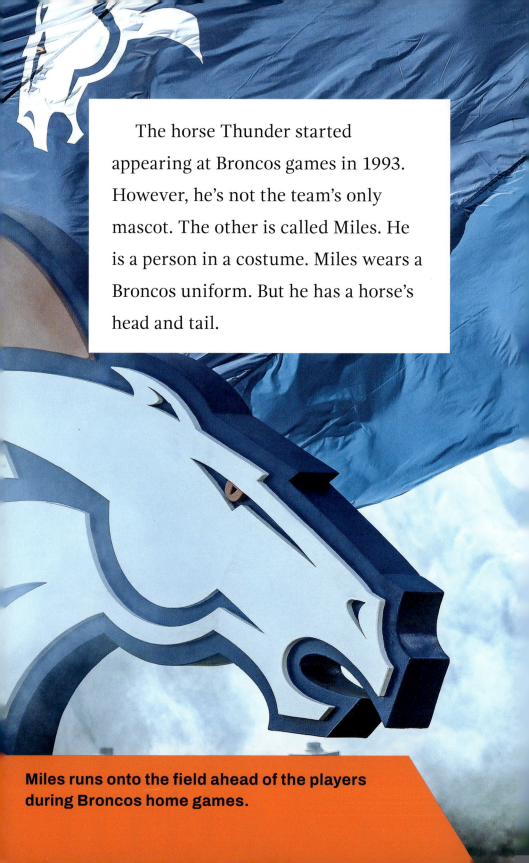

The horse Thunder started appearing at Broncos games in 1993. However, he's not the team's only mascot. The other is called Miles. He is a person in a costume. Miles wears a Broncos uniform. But he has a horse's head and tail.

Miles runs onto the field ahead of the players during Broncos home games.

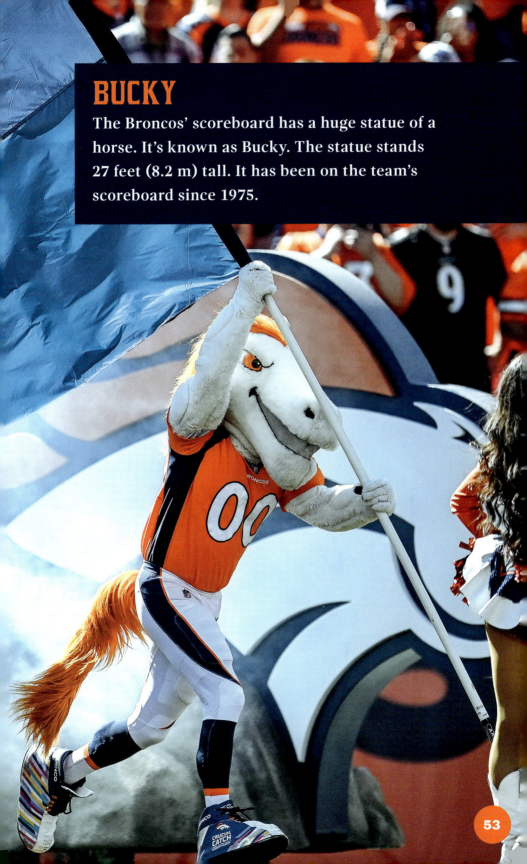

BUCKY

The Broncos' scoreboard has a huge statue of a horse. It's known as Bucky. The statue stands 27 feet (8.2 m) tall. It has been on the team's scoreboard since 1975.

Elway ran for 17 yards in the Super Bowl against the Packers.

John Elway made many big plays for the Broncos. Perhaps the most famous was his "helicopter" play. It happened in the Super Bowl against Green Bay. Elway was trying to run for a first down. He leaped forward. Then he took a big hit. Elway spun around like the blades of a helicopter. But he got the first down. Denver went on to score a touchdown.

TEAM RECORDS

All-Time Passing Yards: 51,475
John Elway (1983–98)

All-Time Touchdown Passes: 300
John Elway (1983–98)

All-Time Rushing Yards: 7,607
Terrell Davis (1995–2001)

All-Time Rushing Touchdowns: 60
Terrell Davis (1995–2001)

All-Time Receiving Yards: 11,389
Rod Smith (1995–2006)

All-Time Interceptions: 44
Steve Foley (1976–86)

All-Time Sacks: 110.5
Von Miller (2011–21)

All-Time Scoring: 1,786
Jason Elam (1993–2007)

All-Time Coaching Wins: 138
Mike Shanahan (1995–2008)

Super Bowl Titles: 3
(1997, 1998, 2015)

All statistics are accurate through 2023.

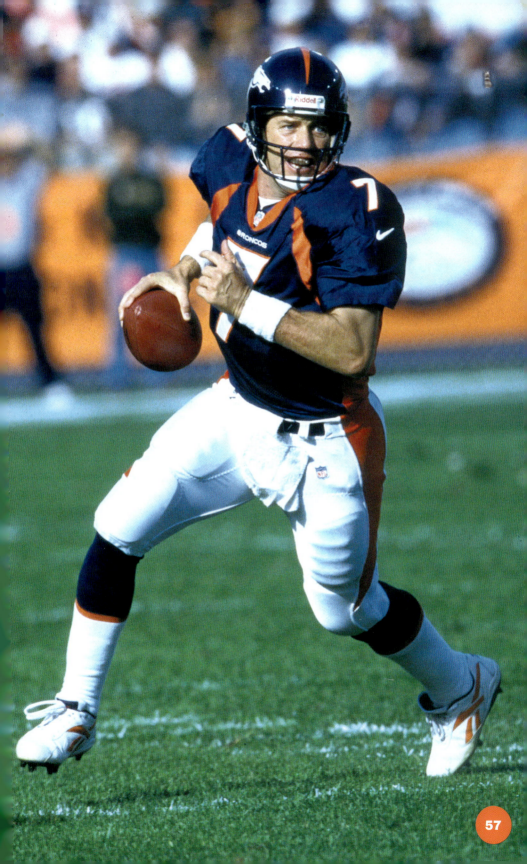

TIMELINE

1960 — The Denver Broncos begin play as members of the AFL.

1977 — The Orange Crush defense leads the Broncos to their first Super Bowl appearance.

1983 — Denver pulls off a trade with the Baltimore Colts to land rookie quarterback John Elway.

1986 — Elway's epic touchdown drive sets up overtime, and the Broncos stun the Cleveland Browns to win the conference championship.

1997 — The Broncos finally win their first Super Bowl with a 31–24 victory over the Green Bay Packers.

1998 — Denver wins the Super Bowl for the second year in a row with a 34–19 victory over the Atlanta Falcons.

2012 — Superstar quarterback Peyton Manning signs with the Broncos.

2013 — Manning sets the single-season NFL record with 55 touchdown passes, but the Broncos fall to the Seattle Seahawks in the Super Bowl.

2015 — In his final NFL game, Manning leads the Broncos to their third Super Bowl title with a 24–10 win over the Carolina Panthers.

2022 — Former Seahawks quarterback Russell Wilson is traded to the Broncos.

COMPREHENSION QUESTIONS

Write your answers on a separate piece of paper.

1. Write a paragraph that explains the main ideas of Chapter 2.

2. Who do you think was the greatest player in Broncos history? Why?

3. Who led Denver to its first Super Bowl win?
    - A. Craig Morton
    - B. John Elway
    - C. Peyton Manning

4. Why might the Broncos' opponents have a hard time playing in Denver?
    - A. The "Mile High Salute" makes it hard to stay focused.
    - B. The "Mile High Thunder" makes it hard to hear play calls.
    - C. New Mile High has a longer playing field than other stadiums.

5. What does **targets** mean in this book?

*Quarterback John Elway led the way. Tight end Shannon Sharpe was one of his favorite **targets**.*

    A. coaches to call plays
    B. defenders to block passes
    C. players to throw to

6. What does **formation** mean in this book?

*Manning often lined up in the shotgun **formation**. When he wanted to change the play, he shouted "Omaha!"*

    A. a play that results in a touchdown
    B. a victory over an easy opponent
    C. the places where players stand before a play starts

Answer key on page 64.

GLOSSARY

conference
A group of teams that make up part of a sports league.

coordinator
An assistant coach who is in charge of the offense, defense, or special teams.

draft
A system that lets teams select new players coming into the league.

league
A group of teams that play one another and compete for a championship.

overtime
An extra period that happens if two teams are tied at the end of the fourth quarter.

playoffs
A set of games played after the regular season to decide which team is the champion.

retired
Ended one's career.

rookie
An athlete in his or her first year as a professional player.

sacks
Plays that happen when a defender tackles the quarterback before he can throw the ball.

shotgun
A formation in which the quarterback begins the play about five yards behind the line of scrimmage.

TO LEARN MORE

BOOKS

Anderson, Josh. *Inside the Denver Broncos.* Minneapolis: Lerner Publications, 2024.

Coleman, Ted. *Denver Broncos All-Time Greats.* Mendota Heights, MN: Press Box Books, 2022.

Greenberg, Keith Elliot. *Patrick Mahomes vs. Peyton Manning: Who Would Win?* Minneapolis: Lerner Publications, 2024.

ONLINE RESOURCES

Visit **www.apexeditions.com** to find links and resources related to this title.

ABOUT THE AUTHOR

Brendan Flynn is a San Francisco resident and an author of numerous children's books. In addition to writing about sports, Flynn also enjoys competing in triathlons, Scrabble tournaments, and chili cook-offs.

INDEX

Alzado, Lyle, 23
Atwater, Steve, 25

Bailey, Champ, 47
Briscoe, Marlin, 23

Davis, Terrell, 27, 28, 48
Dawkins, Brian, 47
Dumervil, Elvis, 45

Elway, John, 14, 17, 18, 27, 30, 35, 55

Harris, Chris, 47

Jackson, Tom, 23

Kubiak, Gary, 35

Little, Floyd, 21

Manning, Peyton, 33, 35–36, 41, 43

Mecklenburg, Karl, 23
Mile High Stadium, 6
Miller, Von, 38, 45
Morton, Craig, 21

Payton, Sean, 36

Romanowski, Bill, 25

Sharpe, Shannon, 27
Smith, Dennis, 25
Smith, Rod, 27
Surtain, Patrick II, 47
Sutton, Courtland, 43

Taylor, Lionel, 21
Thomas, Demaryius, 43

Upchurch, Rick, 25

Ware, DeMarcus, 45
Wilson, Russell, 36

ANSWER KEY:
1. Answers will vary; 2. Answers will vary; 3. B; 4. B; 5. C; 6. C